Venus Anadyomene

poems by

Alyssa Sinclair

Finishing Line Press
Georgetown, Kentucky

Venus Anadyomene

Copyright © 2025 by Alyssa Sinclair
ISBN 979-8-88838-848-8 First Edition
All rights reserved under International and Pan-American Copyright Conventions. No part of this book may be reproduced in any manner whatsoever without written permission from the publisher, except in the case of brief quotations embodied in critical articles and reviews.

ACKNOWLEDGMENTS

Thank you to:

Bear Review for publishing "Three-month portrait of a family" in issue 10.2
Hyacinth Review for publishing "Timecircle" in their Heritage issue
Literary Mama for publishing "Second Baby"
Milk Press for publishing "A prayer" in their Summer 2023 issue
River Teeth for publishing "C-Section" in 'Beautiful Things'
Mutha Magazine for publishing two essays that pre-empted the writing of this collection.

Thank you to my manuscript readers over the years including but not limited to Emily Sinclair, Claudia Cortese and Sarah Carson. Your feedback kept me thinking and evolving.

I would like to thank my wonderful professors at the University of St. Andrews and English teachers over the years, and my parents for the gift of my education. Thank you to my husband Will for supporting and witnessing me through enormous change, recoveries, and transformation over the years.

Publisher: Leah Huete de Maines
Editor: Christen Kincaid
Cover Art: William Sinclair
Author Photo: Robert Sinclair
Cover Design: Elizabeth Maines McCleavy

Order online: www.finishinglinepress.com
also available on amazon.com

Author inquiries and mail orders:
Finishing Line Press
PO Box 1626
Georgetown, Kentucky 40324
USA

Contents

C-Section 1

Ghost Box 2

Unidentified woman, badly decomposed 3

Second baby 5

Sam I Am 6

Vessel 7

Three-month portrait of a family, by CVS pharmacy 8

Uteri in Texas are all over the news 9

Summer's teeth 10

Thirty-two and you drag 11

A prayer 12

Outdoor shower 13

Timecircle 14

Alpha Tauri 15

On the beach 16

A prayer 17

At the edge of the parking lot 18

A car question in Texas 19

A prayer 20

Things said but unsaid by the OB in Dallas 21

A prayer 22

Lover 23

C- Section

Noun; 1) The lights are on bright, the room freezer-cold and strangers wheel you in on a hospital bed, helpless and naked beneath a thin cotton gown, and they stick a needle in your back and you start shaking, from the drugs, cold or panic, who knows, and they lift you from one bed to another on the count of three, slither something through the shining needle in your arm and there is a loud whirring sound, a smell of burning as they cut through skin, your muscles, but (hopefully) not the head of your baby—for that they pull and they twist and POP, out comes a head, and if you're lucky the baby cries, and is taken away to be measured and weighed and ready for somebody else to hold, as the gloved hands push HARD everything back inside, take-your-breath-away hard, terror-hard, and a doctor dictates to another learning-to-be-a-doctor how to stitch up your stomach correctly—and then makes small talk while your insides splay out, numbed out of panic, so very alone after nine months together.

Verb; 2) There is a different kind of silence as the baby is brought back to life, coaxed to breathe, rushed out of the room, a stillness enters that part of you standing open. It is hard to remember what comes next.

Ghost Box

1. The iv drips and clicks and with my eyes closed it could be the eddies of a river. Water over stones, bubblebubbleslick, that tube a tributary running Zofran, Toradol, Dilaudid. It's a drug-runner river, a smoother of pain. The IV Dilaudid goes straight to my brain: pouf.

2. There is servitude in everything. The drug river to the drugs, the drugs to your pain. But the pain, what does the pain serve?

3. A button lives by my left elbow: "Reading", it says, but really it just lifts the shade up and down. This is a main event of the day, looking at the wan winter light over the highway overpasses wondering what time of day it might be out there. Not the time on the clock, but the quality of the day I try to judge by the traffic, the clouds. I miss the first sunset but then the window gives me one that is vivid&glorious. I call it Vivian and Gloria in my head. Vivian and Gloria have an aura of bloodorange, pink.

4. At 6 AM on day two or three I try to shower. All the blood rushes from my head down to my tippy toes. The floor tilts, and suddenly the hospital room is an airplane climbing, climbing to somewhere very alone. Aloneness rings and swirls, a smoky ghost in this white box. Hospital room=ghost box. I make it back to the bed and start to cry because I think I never should have agreed to this procedure. I rip off the plastic sleeve around my IV like I am waxing my arm hair.

5. I have broken out in a clammy sweat. My freshly washed hair is soaking the back of my t-shirt. Feet bare, legs bare; I have run out of clean pajama pants. I am rationing shirts. The adults in my life are taking care of my three children, while I ache for their little bodies. Small backs, long legs, the napes of their necks and velvety backs of their hands that could fit so softly in mine: all as comforting as something sweet that melts in your mouth.

6. A resident comes in and asks, "How are we doing today?" I don't recognize him. Every twelve hours it is someone different. He is thin and young in his whitewhite coat with square pockets. I've turned my body to the window and I can't stop crying. "I should have had a hysterectomy," I say. The pain is a blood red tentacle, live electric wire, a hand in the dark that scratches. "I should have, I never should have done this." The snot is choking me, so I stop talking. He clears his throat. "It will get better," he says, and pats the side of the bed twice before turning away, as if he wants to pat my shoulder, but can't bring himself to. I have never felt so alone.

Unidentified woman, badly decomposed

Police pulled her
from a drainage pipe
by the lake
on the way
to our country club.

I saw her as I drove by—
mauve mottled,
legs flopping,
hair strung and tangled.

Crepe myrtles bloom hot fuchsia in the spring.
They repaved the path,
dredged the silt.

Sometimes the sun
glitters on the surface
of the water beyond
the people jogging
sweat glistening
on their chests
cheeks so flush
and alive
in the shimmering heat
this summer.

Second baby

They peeled back my skin
like onion paper.
A burning smell as they cut
the gristly layers
of fat, sinew,
everything my body
saved for this,
to reveal
what had been living
inside me all along except
she was purple and un-breathing.
Nobody would answer me
from beyond the blue sheet,
crowded as they were
around the ventilator.

Sam I Am

I do not like
green eggs and ham.
I do not like it
Sam I am.
I do not like it
up my skirt
on the bus
dropped his pants
started to jerk.

Would you, could you
on the beach?
I do not like it on the beach.
Would you, could you, on the bed?
I do not like it on the bed.
Do not bump me on the train,
Or make me run in Val Thorens.
Not at 10 PM, on the Lower East Side,
When Sam chased me with his green eggs and

I do not like
ham fingered quick
up my dress at a crowded bar
in New Orleans.
My dress was short,
I was wearing a thong,
then Sam I am
he disappeared.

Vessel

I don't want to hear your happy birth story.
I want to know there isn't something wrong with me,
that I'm not alone in my dysfunctional body that won't let go my
Thank-God-for-modern-medicine-body/ I have never seen a
cervix do this body/ too many hours body/ Epidural body/ Fetal
distress body/ Strapped down, cut open body/ Shaking body/
Breathe into a paper bag body/ Failed VBAC body/ Uterine rupture
body/ Low blood volume body/ Uterine artery embolization
body
That makes people say,
you would've, you could've (died—they whisper)
at least *the baby is healthy*
you should just *be grateful* you're alive.

Three-month portrait of a family, by CVS pharmacy

Amoxicillin Amoxicillin Amoxicillin   *(mox: soon)*
Cephalexin   *(cephal-: head)*
Flo-vent   *(flo: flourish)*
Diazepam Methocarbamol Hydrocodone Trazodone   *(throughout [the]
                                             medicinal, water)*
Amoxicillin Z-Pack   soon soon soon [the]
Amoxicillin
Wellbutrin Desvenlafaxine   desperation
Gabapentin Tramadol Lexapro   of words
Cephalexin Prednisone Azithromycin   *(plunder)ed me*
Cefdinir   *(terribly great)*
Prozac   *(forward movement) [of an]*
Zoloft   *(animal elevated)*
Clonazepam   *(a twig, a spray)*
Cephalexin prednisone *plundered me greatly again*
Alprazolam   (From al(pha) +̂p(henyl) +̂(t)r(i)azol(o)
                                              +̂-(azep)am.
            Countable and uncountable substance
                    To shine
                        A living being
                            (in)to love

Uteri in Texas are all over the news

My legs become a basket when I brush their hair.
They lean their smooth little backs
into the sag of my stomach,
a place to land, curl-in-able, full
of you woven around you, threaded together; my hair is
your hair,
the blue green of
your eyes,
the sky, nail beds and tendons
it's all also

my uterus, that would be the most obvious basket, wouldn't it?
I tell my daughter what a uterus is and she has questions:
Does a *uterus* (she is testing the word out, tasting it) keep the
    baby safe inside?

Can water from the bath get in?
How do doctors know about inside bodies?

This uterus was once
a basket, once
held you, but sliced
now the doctors:
lesioned, bulky, thickened, compromised, unresearched, uncurable

Didn't you do this to me?
You stitched me up.
Now I am stuck inside.

I am 32 but
is there anybody anywhere
that could
hold my weight,
brush my hair,
let me float,
safe inside?

Summer's teeth

Twenty-six, you wander
room to room, baby on your hip.
Texas heat beats on outside.
Bright light concrete.
The air conditioner drones and hums
the song of a long, uphill battle.

It is too hot to walk, to eat, to think.
Too, too, too.
Nascent anxiety peels, curls around you.
Your parents call and ask, *When will you come?*
You tell them, *I have a life here now.*
There are empty rooms, extra rooms, blank closets full of promise—

Thirty-two and you drag

yourself outside with all three children dreading
the way your black SUV heats up like a personal pre-heated oven.
They love to swim but you want them to know there is more to life than this:
ketchup stains like smeared blood on bleach white towels.
hot concrete chlorine that kills everything alive and dries
into a stale sweaty smell on swimsuits strewn like shed skins
limp and lifeless in the laundry room,

In the car after, your six-year-old asks, "Is summer here a whole year long?"
You laugh. She says, "When you really don't enjoy something, it feels very slow."

A prayer

Tall angel, please,
Drip honey off your fingertips into the mouths of
My children, and deliver them from
This air-conditioned life
into something
more alive.

Outdoor shower

The soaring blue sky. Water sluiced down the oak planks, perpetually slick, growing algae, slices of the strawberry patch showing through the cracks. The water pooled in our tiny, grainy handprints in the cement—or were those the handprints of my mother and her brothers? The runoff—shampoo, sand, sunscreen—formed a tiny creek that ran toward the garden bed my father built, long gone now, where zucchini plants and peppers grew and my mother broke her leg one afternoon, no doubt teetering on the edge as she picked something for dinner. She was pregnant that summer. After that, she hobbled to the beach on crutches. We followed, 1, 2, 3 children, our warm towels draped around our necks like flags.

Timecircle

I spiral back
to the center of myself.
In woods thick with
ferns, blueberry, sassafras, thorns, poison ivy.
Pine needles, dead leaves, hairy moss beneath bare feet.
Rocks push through soft soil blooming.
I tear open a wintergreen,
fall backwards to the center of time.
I was a child in this place.
> *Did you know that plant smells like toothpaste*
> *ferns are the plant version of feathers and*
> *lady slippers turn to fairies in the night?*
Rhubarb and root beer floats
inhabit sassafras.
I knew all the boulders throughout these woods,
now shrinking in the overgrowth,

The ocean opens vastly beneath the bluff,
the horizon a glowing line.
Opaque cloudwall,
Toes in loamy dirt,
Towering pines sway so much
I wonder if they might be dead or dying now—
everything once so huge reveals itself as
possibly, probably,
fragile after all.

Alpha Tauri

My childhood boat, a bull's eye,
sleeps between pines,
head bowed, a wrinkled
blue tarp its comforter.

Aldebaran, my grandmother named it,
"For my favorite bull"
I thought it was back in Arizona,

but now I know she meant,
rose star, eye
of the bull, archangel
victorious constellation more luminous
than the sun.

When I was a child, its heavy hull was
unflappable, life jacket strapped,
salt on lips, it crossed the wind
with so much certainty.
Vessel of strength, protector of children,
bearer of wishes, of memory,
Aldebaran.

On the beach

Reiterations of shell after shell,
shards of bone,
left behind gristle, feathers:
the sand itself
a wistful list
of brokenness.

Eye of the oyster,
a bruise tucked in the curve,
watching, watching—
Do you remember being split open,
wet, alive,
throbbing, indignant,
before the winter, the water, the wind,
turned you weather-worn,
chalky, distant,
almost smooth, almost
a semblance
of yourself?

A prayer

Let the violet iridescent mussels,
partner-bound with a last thread
of sinew, become clackers
in the hands of my children.

At the edge of the parking lot

A bright new sign
at my daughter's school shines
beyond the black-eyed susans'
upturned faces, the crimson poppy
flock of warbling necks,
the echinacea and sage silvering
in the morning light:
oficial de policía
en la Propiedad

A car question in Texas

"What do you do when you don't want a baby?"

It is 110 degrees Fahrenheit, feels like 115.
I open the car door.
The humidity and the heat
is a steam press and I am
a sheet being smoothed out into nothing.
The pressure is so great
the inside of my head is
a collapsing bridge.

I am pleating into
a place behind the heatwall.
I try to gather the edges back up
into a semblance of safety
as we file inside,
1, 2, 3
girls and me.

The cicadas rattle like a *cascabel*;
a warning bell,
a cannon.

A prayer

Tall angel,
Braid and oil the hair
of my children.
Make it waves of
bequeathed wishes.
Tomorrow, make it a fortress.
Let the the bluesad glow
of this bentneck world
run off their strength
like rain on a duck's back,
like summer sweat
washed away
like nothing.

Things said but unsaid by the OB in Dallas

Heels in cold ribbed stirrups,
where tongue meets throat
I taste the metallic drip of your fear.
Oblong wand, smothered in jelly—
I shiver from your desperation.

A prayer

Black swallowtail, as big as a bird,
with your jagging wing,
and uncertain beating,
Bless my children.

Old tree wearing
the skin of the universe,
protect this quiet
star moss driveway.
Help us be still enough to hear
your harbored history,
the bloom of ochre lichen
at your side, your fallen, laced leaf
resting—

Lover

The only way I know
to keep the ocean is to swallow
its meat, slick the brine,
let it soften, stew
become my skin, my hair,
my longing. Still, I crave
lapping at my ankles,
a misty caress,
a hush-hush song,
the steadfast work,
or else, a spitting temper.

These days,
it's the only one who brings me gifts,
of shells, bones, glass,
turned over so many times,
worry turns to memory,
to cryptic etchings, to old tales
of life and death.

Today, I have no ocean
to swallow and ache
for lavender thrift, sea oats bending
their heads in prayer,
to be surrounded by a wordless garden
of myth, the certain meter of time rising
around my ankles.

Alyssa Lindley Sinclair earned her Master's degree in Creative Writing at the University of St. Andrews, where she also completed an undergraduate degree in Art History. She grew up in the Boston area, and currently lives in Dallas, Texas. She is the mother to three young girls and has been the primary caregiver to her children for the past eight years. Her poetry and essays have been most recently featured by *Bear Review, River Teeth Journal, Mutha Magazine, Literary Mama, The Hyacinth Review, Blueline Magazine,* Poetry Society of New York, and she was Pushcart Prize nominated in 2024. This is her first chapbook of poetry.

Venus Anadyomene chronicles the trauma endured by a women's body, while exploring the intersection of mental and physical health, the threat of climate change, the political landscape in Texas, and a mother's longing for a safer and more beautiful existence for her children. Alyssa's next project continues to explore hybrid forms of poetry, the intersection of body, psyche and landscape, and the junction of spirituality meeting the mundane.

Find out more at: *byalyssasinclair.com*

www.ingramcontent.com/pod-product-compliance
Lightning Source LLC
Chambersburg PA
CBHW022108080426
42734CB00009B/1514